SHADOWS AND SUBSTANCE

GW00771572

Series Editor: MEIC STEPHENS

Shadows and Substance

The Development of a Media Policy for Wales

Kevin Williams

First Impression—March 1997

ISBN 1 85902 453 X

Printed in Wales at
Gomer Press, Llandysul, Ceredigion

Why should anyone in Wales be concerned about what the press, television and radio are saying about them? Welsh people are confronted by many problems: unemployment, rural depopulation, poverty, rising drug abuse and alcoholism, falling provision of education, poor housing, the growth of crime and violence to the person, environmental degradation, the increased cost of the basic needs of life, light, heat and water and so on. It seems an indulgence to talk about the role of the mass media in representing what it means to be Welsh amid such problems. Often discussion of our national and cultural identity is made without reference to the quality of the daily life of many of our fellow women and men. It neglects the real problems that exist in the streets and fields of Wales. But the importance of the mass media is the crucial role they play in how we make sense of these problems and understand our plight and that of our fellow citizens. The people of Penrhys in the Rhondda recently reminded us of the importance of representation when, in a rare departure, they were allowed by BBC Wales to have a 'right of reply' to a BBC 2 documentary about their community. Being incarcerated in someone else's misrepresentation of your life or community can be a withering form of imprisonment. Any discussion of the mass media and Welsh identity should be grounded firmly in the concerns of the people of Wales, in all their shapes and sizes.

The mass media play a central role in the construction of Welsh identity, what it means to be Welsh in today's rapidly changing world. The blurb on the cover of John Davies's recent official biography of BBC Wales states that 'contemporary Wales is an artefact produced by broadcasting'. Whether you accept this sweeping assessment or not, the media are the main means by which Wales represents itself to the outside world as well as defining what it is to be Welsh to the people who live in Wales. For many the development of strong indigenous mass media is an essential step to challenging the misrepresentation of Wales by the London media. Voices are regularly raised against the most blatant forms of stereotyping to which Wales is subjected in the UK media and many argue that the more Welsh broadcasters and writers are allowed access to the UK media, the better Wales is able to represent itself to the rest of Britain. But the development of indigenous media is also important in allowing people in Wales to build and foster their own sense of identity. Through the mass media we can explore and examine what it means to be Welsh. Mass media of our own are not only important in combatting the stereotyping of Welsh identity by others but also vital ingredients in the building of collective solidarity and understanding inside Wales, and addressing the problems that we face as a community.

The importance of the growth of Welsh media structures is accentuated by the rapid changes that are occurring both inside and outside Wales. The traditional modes of economic production that have underpinned Welsh culture are quickly disappearing. As pits have closed, steel works disappeared and communities dwindled, the traditional Welsh way of life has evaporated. Wales is no longer able to represent itself through its chapels, coal mines and rugby football. New forms of expression are needed for the next century. But the outside world is also changing. The old certainties of national media systems are being eroded by the winds of technological change. A global inform-ation and communication revolution is happening which could transform not only social relations but the main mechanisms by which we communicate. Traditional media systems based on mass production for mass audiences are being challenged by new media technologies which are threatening to sweep away national boundaries. In the midst of such changes it is important to build media structures in Wales which represent who we are and what we stand for in the modern world.

The final factor in the importance of developing Welsh media is the promise of a devolution of power and government within the United Kingdom if the Labour Party wins the next election. If devolution is to work it is important that popular support is built for a Welsh Parliament or Assembly. Too often in the past support for a Welsh Assembly from politicians and leading intellectuals has been mistaken for popular backing for such a development. If an Assembly is to work in future it will need broad-based support from the people of Wales and the mass media will play an essential

6

part in building that support. But the politics of devolution should not be seen solely in a United Kingdom context. Wales — as the rest of the United Kingdom — is part of a changing Europe. The New Europe is envisaged as a 'Europe of the Regions' and if Wales is to have its voice heard within these new structures it will need to develop its sense of identity.

There are a number of reasons why the development of indigenous media is important to modern Wales and its problems. Yet the debate about the role the mass media should and do play in Welsh society has by and large been limited. For most of the last decade there has been little discussion of the extent to which the media are effective in their representation of Wales at home and abroad. What passes for discussion has been confined to those who work in the media, aided and often abetted by politicians. The lack of a critical culture inside Wales has further retarded discussion. The review columns of the leading newspaper in Wales — *The Western Mail* — spend less and less space on reviewing the content of Welsh radio and television. In the last year what have passed for review columns have been replaced by a special arts and entertainment supplement in which plugs and puffs for programmes have replaced any critical evaluation of what the media and cultural industries are producing. Broadcasting itself spends little time examining what goes on behind its own doors and many in the arts reflect traditional intellectual disdain for the mass media. There has almost been a conspiracy of silence around the output of the Welsh media and assessments of the 'quality' have been built around the views of the few and their interpretation of what Welsh people want and like to see on their television screens, read in their newspapers and listen to on their radios.

This booklet hopes to make a small contribution to raising some debate about the role of the mass media in building a future for a modern Wales. It provides an overview of recent developments in the Welsh media and examines some of the arguments that have emerged about how best to develop the Welsh media to meet the needs and requirements of the new millennium as well as to reflect the problems that face Welsh people and Welsh society. It also makes a number of suggestions as to the way forward. These suggestions are made with one overriding concern in mind—unless there are radical changes in Wales in the near future then we are living through the last years of our way of life, our culture. Despite all the changes in the institutional landscape of Wales, from the Welsh Office to the Konica League of Wales, which appear to provide a more concrete expression of our collective identity, much of the contemporary observations of what is happening in Wales are part and parcel of documenting decline. As institutions emerge, the sense of what it means to be Welsh is becoming more problematic. There is a crisis of consciousness of who we are, what we stand for, where we came from and in particular where we are going. This is nothing new, some would say. When was Wales? There has always been a problem with what it means to be Welsh. But today that problem is more acute than ever and without a concerted attempt to rebuild and re-establish a political and cultural consciousness of Welshness, the Welsh people threaten to fall off the edge of the modern world map. In the late twentieth century the mass media are the 'consciousness industries' and it is to them that we must turn for a lead in the development of new identities to replace those that have disappeared and to set the agenda for discussing the pressing issues of the day.

A slice of Welsh media history

Where better to begin than with history? Wales is a land of historians, picking over the embers of a hazy past. Much of this picking has been done on our television screens where history men (most of them are) have done endless pieces to camera reclaiming a variety of aspects of our past. As yet our television screens have not witnessed the reclaiming of the history of the Welsh media, and the role these industries have played in the process by which we have come to know about ourselves. Perhaps the main reason for this is that the most significant feature of the history of the Welsh media has been their failure to establish

8

themselves as national entities. Wales has never had a national newspaper. The newspaper industry in Wales in the 19th century, as Aled Jones has documented[1], was highly localised — a stark contrast with England, Scotland and Ireland where the print industry grew up in and expanded from the major conurbations of Glasgow, Edinburgh, London and Dublin.

It has only been in the 20th century that efforts have been made to appeal beyond locality to address the Welsh nation as a whole. *The Western Mail* throughout its history has made the most concerted effort to reach a national audience through the medium of the English language. By the early 1960s it had established itself in South, West and, to some extent, East Wales. However, it never achieved any significant penetration into North Wales - and was never able to live up to its logo's claim to be the 'national newspaper of Wales'. Readership of *The Western Mail* in the 'sixties and 'seventies was high among both Welsh and English-speakers; its heyday was in the early 1960s when its circulation rose to around 104,000. Readers might have been critical of its editorial line — and there were often complaints about the nature of its news coverage — but the paper was read because it provided a relatively wide range of reports on Welsh affairs.

The rest of the English-language daily press was by and large established in the highly populated conurbations of South Wales— Swansea, Cardiff and Newport. North Wales is served by the Liverpool *Daily Post* which through its Welsh edition has claimed to be 'speaking up for Wales'. The best-read newspapers in Wales, however, have always been London newspapers with the *Sun* and the *Daily Mirror* taking the lead. Based on 1995 figures the *Sun* has the highest degree of household penetration in Wales (22.5%). *The Western Mail* reaches only 6% of Welsh households. Only 13% of newspapers read in Wales are produced in the country, which contrasts sharply with the situation in Scotland where the figure is nearly 90%. Wales is also a tabloid-reading nation with the readership of the tabloids being nearly ten times greater than that of the 'quality' press.[2] There has also never been a successful national daily newspaper in the Welsh language — as is the case with most of Europe's 'lesser-used languages'.

According to Dylan Iorwerth, this can be attributed to the 'psychological blockage' Welsh-speakers face when it comes to reading in their language. There is an assumption in Welsh-speaking Wales that the 'written culture is essentially in English', which reflects the attitude of many European minority language speakers to the use of their own mother-tongue.[3]

The fight to establish a separate national broadcasting service for Wales has perhaps been fought more keenly than the attempt to establish a national newspaper. In this struggle Wales has always been pitted not only against London but also the West Country — an area whose hostility to things Welsh can never be over-estimated. It was not until 1937 that a separate Welsh Home Service of BBC radio was set up. This was in part the product of a campaign led by Saunders Lewis against *Bradwr Budr Cymru* (BBC) — 'dirty betrayer of Wales' — which in his opinion administered Wales as a 'conquered region'. Ironically the crucial pressure which led the BBC to set up a separate Welsh service came not from Wales but from the West of England which complained of having to share a wavelength with Wales. The *Bristol Evening World* in 1931, for example, aired the grievances of many West Country people about having to listen to 'services from obscure Welsh chapels'. The paper called for the divorce of the two areas by stating that the 'West wants wireless home rule'.[4] The BBC in Wales has always been firmly part of the Corporation, a 'national region' in an organization that has throughout most of its career vigorously pursued a policy of making the people of the United Kingdom all part of one *British* happy family.

Commercial TV was introduced into the British Isles with a mandate to reflect life in the 'regions'. However, it had an even more difficult time establishing itself in Wales. The birth of ITV was a shambles in Wales. Wales West and North (WWN), which began broadcasting in September 1962, became the only ITV company to go out of business. A number of technical, cultural and financial reasons have been cited for this débâcle but the main reason was that the audience was already receiving ITV programmes from Cardiff and Manchester. It was in fact Granada that produced the first Welsh-language programmes while South

10

Wales was served by Television West and Wales (TWW), which produced programmes for the West of England, South Wales and Welsh-speakers in Wales. This situation reflected the view of those in charge of ITV that the population of Wales was too small to sustain a commercial channel through advertising. The poverty and low purchasing power of Wales has been the major factor in the resistance to setting up an independent TV channel serving Wales alone. The arrival of Harlech Television (HTV), which took over the franchise for Wales and the West region in 1968, did see a greater commitment to Wales — at least on paper with the names of many of Wales's greatest cultural patriots supporting the company. In commercial broadcasting terms, however, Wales has never been treated as a national entity — it has never been able to shake off the economic shackles placed on it by its relationship with the West Country.

The history of the Welsh press and broadcasting up until the late 1970s highlights the deep ambivalence of Welsh people to their own culture. The failure to produce a strong surge of support for a national newspaper and broadcasting channels represents an inferiority complex which has characterized what we feel and believe about the value of our culture. Despite the continual clamouring about the inequities and injustices that the London media heap on efforts to represent Wales and Welshness, there is an underlying insecurity about whether we have anything worthwhile to represent to the outside world. It is this mindset as much as the economic, technical and political obstacles that has held back the development of indigenous media in Wales.

A comparison with Scotland

The failure of the Welsh media to establish themselves as national institutions led the sociologist Jeremy Tunstall to state that the 'Welsh media are much less Welsh than the Scottish media are Scottish'.[5] Comparison is often made with Scotland in discussing the role of the media in the development of national consciousness in Wales. Scotland has a thriving national newspaper industry. Scottish broadsheet newspapers such as the *Herald* and the *Scotsman* outsell the combined strength of all the English quality press in Scotland. The *Daily Record* at the tabloid end of the market sells daily on average 750,000. Even local and regional newspapers such as the *Courier* in Dundee and the Aberdeen *Press and Journal* sell around 111,000 and 108,000 respectively. Recently the *Sun* was renamed north of the border the *Scottish Sun*, and between 1987 and 1994 it doubled its sales by stressing its commitment to Scottish independence and producing more Scottish material. The strength of the Scottish press is seen by some in Wales as something to envy. Through its press, some argue, Scotland has been able to develop a more clearly defined sense of political consciousness than Wales.

It is the case that over two-thirds of Scots read newspapers published, printed and edited in Scotland. However, comparison between Wales and Scotland must be carefully made. Maurice Smith[6] in his recent book *Paper Lions* makes a number of observations about the role of the national press in the construction of Scottish consciousness. Despite the logo commitments to serving Scotland on the masthead of the leading Scottish newspapers, they only sell well in their immediate regions or areas. For example, more than 80% of the readership of the *Herald* is confined to the Strathclyde region whereas nearly 50% of the *Scotsman*'s readership is in the Lothian region centred on Edinburgh. These papers with national pretensions are nearly matched in terms of total sales by newspapers such as the Aberdeen *Press and Journal* and the Dundee *Courier* which are unashamedly committed to their locality. For Smith, most of the Scottish press can be described as 'city state' newspapers which give a clear voice to the sharp regional differences within Scotland. For example, the *Press and Journal* was highly sceptical of renewed calls for greater independence for Scotland in the 1990s, representing the traditional concerns in the North East of Scotland about 'control from Edinburgh'. Thus the Scottish press often articulates regional and local identities at the expense of national consciousness. Perhaps the lesson to draw from Scotland is that political and national consciousness are strong enough to allow the Scottish press to articulate the regional and local differences within Scottish society. This contrasts with Wales where the weakness of Welsh consciousness accentuates concerns over the failure of newspapers to articulate national sentiments and feelings.

The emergence of a Welsh media system

Since the early 1980s there has been a rapid growth in the media industries in Wales, which it is argued is leading to the emergence for the first time of a distinct national media system. This growth has been led by the broadcasting institutions. The first development was the decision in 1977 to split BBC radio in Wales into two channels broadcasting in Welsh and English. Radio Cymru broadcasts approximately 75 hours per week and Radio Wales about 110 hours. The division of radio set the pattern for broadcasting in the 1980s. The most significant step forward was the setting up of *Sianel Pedwar Cymru* (S4C) in 1982. Both Radio Cymru and S4C treat Wales as a distinct nation. Ian Hume in his study of content of the broadcast media in Wales in 1984/5 shows that the 'broadcast media in the Welsh language appear to have a relatively clear identity, linked to a perception of Wales as a spatially defined political, social and cultural entity'.[7] This is done by providing Welsh-speakers with a Welsh perspective on international affairs through current affairs programmes such as *Y Byd ar Bedwar* and *Taro Naw* as well as feature programmes and dramas which represent popular culture and life in Wales. The fact that this has been developed in the Welsh language should not be a surprise as Welsh-speaking Wales has always been more conscious of Wales as a nation than its English-speaking counter-parts. A report in 1991 commissioned by the Institute of Welsh Affairs found that a greater percentage of Welsh-speakers were more supportive of an English-language TV channel for Wales than English-speakers.[8]

The presence of S4C has, however, also provided the impetus for the growth of English-language television in Wales. Following the advent of S4C both HTV and BBC Wales have appeared to give more time to issues of Welsh national significance. The fact that both BBC and HTV are making programmes for S4C has, it can be argued, resulted in a more Wales-orientated approach in the production values throughout the whole of Welsh broadcasting. The success of S4C in serving the needs of Welsh-speakers led to calls for an English-language TV service for Wales. While such a service has not materialised it is certainly true that BBC Wales and HTV have produced a 'new deal' for English-language television in Wales. Both channels have devoted more attention to Wales in the 1980s with an increase of their English-language output to about ten hours each a week. This is an important point because despite all the criticisms levelled at the channel, it is S4C that has been the catalyst in the emergence of a distinct Welsh broadcasting system.

There have also been changes in the print media. *Wales on Sunday*, a new English-language Sunday newspaper in Wales, was launched in 1989 in recognition of Wales's 'over-dependence on the London press'.[9] After a shaky start the newspaper has established itself as one of the fastest-growing papers in Britain with a circulation of around 62,000. This contrasts with its sister paper, *The Western Mail*, which has seen a steady decline in circulation since 1979. Today its circulation stands at 68,456. Similar declines in circulation are seen with the rest of the major newspapers printed in Wales. The most striking change since 1979 has been the emergence of community newspapers, especially the Welsh-language *papurau bro*. These monthly newspapers began in the mid-1970s and there are now 52 of them with a circulation of around 72,000.[10] Free newspapers have also proliferated. It is now estimated that there are 50 of these with considerable circulations — the *Cardiff Independent*, for example, boasted a weekly circulation of 110,000.[11]

Since 1979 there has been an increase in the quantity of media in Wales, that is media made in Wales, by Welsh people and for the Welsh and English-speakers of Wales. This is a positive development but the foundations of Welsh media institutions are far from secure and more significantly there are a number of features of the emerging media system which call into question their ability, capacity and willingness to develop a sense of national consciousness and identity in Wales.

Not waving but drowning?

The growth of Welsh media institutions is another example of the development of government and non-government organizations in Wales which has begun to give the nation an identity beyond that of language. This is something that we can applaud but if these institutions are not built on the foundations of strong popular support then they can and will be blown away as quickly as they were established. It is the role of the media to build this support and develop a sense of national consciousness. But is it able to? There are several features of this emerging media system that prevent the Welsh media from making a stronger contribution to the development of a Welsh national consciousness.

The decline of the Welsh press

The first feature of the contemporary media landscape in Wales is the increasingly marginal role of the press. The press in Wales, never particularly strong, is today in decline. The decline is happening not only here at home but elsewhere in Britain and the world. New media technology and cultural changes are now beginning to signal an end to literary culture. People appear to be reading less, and in particular are reading fewer newspapers. This is most pronounced amongst young people; in the last British newspaper readership survey only 59% of young people between the ages of 16 and 24 said they read a newspaper. Younger people, weaned in a more visual culture, say that they do not find reading a newspaper a pleasurable activity. Television is today the main source of information for most people about what is going on in the world around them. Faced with the dominance of television, newspapers have been forced into one of two options: to focus more on providing analysis of the context to the news and information that appears on television or to depart from seeing newspapers as a source of information and concentrate on providing entertainment. The result is a polarization in the British press between 'quality' broadsheets and the 'tabloids'. Within the 'provincial press' — that is newspapers published outside London — with some notable exceptions the trend has been towards producing lighter, more entertainment-orientated newspapers with a greater emphasis on colour and eye-catching graphics as well as more lifestyle and human interest stories to make reading a newspaper appeal to the younger audience who are vital to their long-term survival. Thus newspaper reading is in decline and what people are reading in their newspapers has changed considerably in the last decade or so.

These changes are apparent in the fate of Wales's leading newspaper, *The Western Mail*. In the late 1970s the newspaper decided to reposition itself in the market by placing equal emphasis on reporting news from Britain, Wales and abroad; the aim was to produce a newspaper which would cater for all the reader's interests. He or she would not have to buy another newspaper to obtain news about something not covered in *The Western Mail*. The Welsh reader was identified in this change as someone with an equal interest in what is happening in Britain and abroad as well as here in Wales — not an unreasonable assumption considering the overwhelming rejection of the 1979 Devolution Bill in Wales and the country's lurch to the right at the General Election that same year. The newspaper also seemed to attempt to become more broadsheet in its orientation. However, this change did not appear to be accompanied by a commitment to increasing resources needed to run a quality broadsheet with detailed analysis of what was happening in Wales, Britain and the rest of the world. The paper continued to experience financial difficulties, accentuated by the new demands placed on the staff. Falling circulation and advertising revenue led to cutbacks with fewer pages and reporters. As a result there was a squeeze on Welsh news and coverage of our national events. Recent attempts have been made to change the newspaper back to identifying more with its readership's Welshness. Talk of the newspaper going tabloid apparently fell by the wayside when market research found this to be unpopular not only with readers but with advertisers. The relaunched broadsheet paper trumpeted its policy of being 'Welsh with attitude'. This has not, however, produced much more news about Wales — although recently the newspaper's features have concentrated on providing a more all-Wales angle. But news is largely local news about Wales with all-Welsh news, so important to the sense of national consciousness, marginal.

The trend towards less all-Wales news is also apparent in the other newspaper which claims a large readership in Wales. Ian Hume, in his study of the content of the media in Wales in the early 1980s, concluded that 'there is little in the English language press — particularly the weeklies — which offers any support to the idea that Wales is a distinct nation'.[12] Since Hume's study little appears to have changed except for the growth in the rhetorical commitment to all-Wales news. The Liverpool *Daily Post* has made a great effort in recent years to be 'The Paper for Wales'. It has expanded its news-gathering operation in Wales and even appointed a Welsh Affairs correspondent. In the run-up to the recent twenty-fifth anniversary of the investiture of Prince Charles, the newspaper emphasised its 'commitment' to Wales. In a commentary piece to accompany a special 12-page supplement assessing the Prince's role in Wales, the *Post*'s editor highlighted the newspaper's coverage of Welsh issues compared with the London dailies. While all the Fleet Street newspapers together carried only 19 stories about Wales on June 23rd, his newspaper had more than 60 news, business and sports stories from Wales. Such coverage, according to the *Post*'s editor, shows how the newspaper puts the readers and advertisers of Wales first. However, many of these stories are not national Welsh stories but highly localised, emanating from traditional institutional sources such as the courts and councils around the country.

Wales on Sunday has perhaps made the greatest effort to provide an all-Wales coverage. The newspaper was first launched as a quality broadsheet with a specific commitment to providing more all-Welsh news and commentaries. However, the newspaper struggled from the outset; after selling the first edition to 97,000 people, it saw its circulation decline rapidly. It was only after its reincarnation as a tabloid, positioned somewhere between the *Mail on Sunday* and the *Sunday Mirror*, that it began to achieve some success. Welsh stories were still important as the editor spelled out in 1993: ' I'll give them [the readers] a choice with a good Welsh story. What I do is make us a good second buy'.[13] He also continued to place emphasis on crusading journalism, calling his paper the 'campaigning voice of Wales'. But one casualty of the change was the serious attention given by the newspaper to the cultural, political and social life of Wales. The tabloid paper concentrates more on lifestyles and entertainment features, personalities, gossip and fashion. Welsh news stories are there but the focus is primarily on human interest stories and they are lost amongst the welter of lifestyle features and commentaries. The claim to be a campaigning newspaper is also far from convincing. As one former *Wales on Sunday* reporter said: 'The paper's investigative stories have no substance. They are superficial. You think you are in for a good read but the story simply runs out of steam'. This is not a surprise as good investigative journalism requires a lot of staff, money and time, which *Wales on Sunday*, like other newspapers in Wales, does not have.

The trend towards local news in the Welsh press is highlighted by the success of community and local weekly papers in Wales in the 1980s — in both the Welsh and English language. In addition newspapers such as the *South Wales Argus* and *South Wales Evening Post*, which have placed more emphasis on news about their locality, have been better able to arrest — or at least slow down — the decline in circulation. This indicates that Welsh readers today are as firmly — if not more — attached to their locality as to the nation. What this means is that the press in Wales, faced with an increasingly competitive market, is less committed to a national agenda — the exception being parts of the Welsh-language press, most notably *Golwg*. Newspapers might have the resources and inclination to gather news around Wales but not about Wales. The lack of a national dimension has been

18

acknowledged by the *papurau bro* with the establishment of *Cymdeithas y Papurau Bro*, the aim of which is to exchange information and news between the fifty or so newspapers. A success in strict financial terms — as well as important to the maintenance of the Welsh language — these papers are also an example of the failure of the press in Wales to develop a national agenda. And if our own newspapers are less committed to reporting Welsh news then we have little grounds for complaining about the decline of the coverage of Wales in the British press over the last decade.

Welsh TV — representing whom?

For most people today a sense of what Wales is, what it wants to be and what problems it faces is something that comes from the telly. Television is the main source of information about what is happening in the world for most people in Wales. In recent years both BBC Wales and HTV have reiterated that the role of television in Wales is not only to provide information and entertainment but also to play a significant role in the development of Welsh identity. The BBC Controller has recently made the firm commitment that 'BBC Wales's programme agenda should be dominated by that which is significant to the lives of the people of Wales'[14]. Similarly HTV, in its struggle to retain the ITV franchise, emphasised that its mission was 'to unify Wales'. Or in the words of Huw Davies, the then Director of Television for HTV, the raison d'être of the company was 'the reinforcement of our identity; to present the Welsh to the Welsh and to be proud, in so far as it is justifiable, of who we are'. Broadcasting in Wales then is seen as having a cultural mission.

However, the Welsh TV nation speaks with two tongues and this presents obstacles to the broadcasters' attempts to realise their cultural goals. For Welsh-speakers there is a full and comprehensive service. Despite criticism about the size of its viewing figures and the cost of the service, S4C is by and large popular with its audience. Nearly a quarter of all Welsh-speakers claim to watch the channel more often than they watch network television. The channel offers a range of programmes from news and current affairs, documentaries and dramas, to soaps and farming programmes and comedies and quiz shows, all of which achieve a high penetration of their potential audience.[15] The status of the language has been assisted by the channel's existence and S4C has played a significant part in the development of other cultural industries in Wales. Over the years there has been criticism from some parts of the Welsh-speaking audience that their needs have not been fully met — for example, from Welsh youth. There have also been criticisms about the kind of product served up by the channel. The emphasis on the language has sometimes meant that insufficient attention has been paid to programme content. Ned Thomas has drawn attention to programmes on S4C that 'lack a Welsh perspective': he asserts that language is not the only criterion for a programme being Welsh but also form and context.[16] However, overall the channel has 'solid support' from the Welsh-speaking community.

For English-speaking Welsh people the television service is patchy and dotted throughout the schedule. The setting up of S4C did encourage BBC Wales and HTV Wales to devote more attention to providing programmes for English-speakers. However, the expansion of the English-language output of Welsh television has been slow and not to the satisfaction of many. The most parochial of the English-speaking Welsh in those parts of Wales that cannot receive Channel Four UK have been vociferous in demanding their 'rights' to view the London-based station. The quality of the programmes produced for English-language television in Wales has been subject to criticism. Some have argued that 'much of the quality of the increased output from both BBC Wales and HTV Wales has been poor bordering on the downright bad'.[17] Up until recently much of the weekly output of BBC and HTV Wales in English has been taken up by news, current affairs and sport. BBC has recently devoted more time, money and attention to news and current affairs, appointing specialist correspondents to more fully and expertly cover Wales on a regular basis on both radio and television. HTV has also

20

recently revamped its evening news programme, *Wales Tonight*, which is now broadcast at the same time as BBC *Wales Today* — perhaps an unnecessary duplication in light of the limited time given over to English-language Welsh television material.

There are also questions about what kind of Welsh news we are provided with. Television news in Wales — as elsewhere around the world — is becoming more entertainment orientated. The emphasis in the changes in the recently revamped *Wales Today* is on style and presentation. One news presenter instead of two, the layout of the studio and colour of the backdrop as well as the importance of 'live' links with reporters around Wales, have all been mentioned by the BBC as important aspects of the new programme. 'Live' television is seen as something that the viewers want but in the case of the live links on *Wales Today* the new technology to bring us such coverage is wasted. It takes a vivid imagination — and the use of the word 'live' on screen — to distinguish between live images of reporters standing in front of hospitals or other such buildings and pre-recorded images of reporters standing in front of hospitals or other such buildings. What there is less talk about is the content of the programme. Both BBC and HTV news are dominated by local stories about Wales with an emphasis on crime, accidents and sport. BBC Wales, perhaps, has made a greater effort to provide an all-Wales angle on the news but often such reporting is trapped within the 'worthy' traditions of the Corporation. Ultimately English-language broadcast news reporting struggles to make sense and understand what it thinks its audience wants. Radio news exemplifies the problem of responding to a Welsh audience. Radio Wales both in its morning and early news magazine programmes struggles to find a happy mean between local news, all-Wales news and British news. The main thrust of the programmes seems to be on Welsh presenters relaying British national news stories with the occasional Welsh or Wales-based 'expert' commenting on the event. Such reporting locates the listener as being first and foremost part of a British audience.

Apart from news, current affairs and sport there is a mish mash of programmes. In response to the Controller's lament in 1991 that 'about 85% of our present eight hours a week of English language output is news, current affairs and sport, that is reactive programming or topical programming geared to specific events', BBC Wales television has started to invest more in the production of drama, music, documentaries and the arts.[18] HTV is trying to produce more light entertainment, children's and family programming with local entertainers. It is possible to argue that in the 'nineties there has been a polarisation in the output of the two channels. The trend in HTV Cymru/Wales is towards more 'pap television' while BBC Wales is developing more 'patrician' broadcasting. HTV Wales since 1991 has brought us cheap magazine programmes such as *Get Going* which dealt with leisure activities including 'flower arranging, cookery and water colour painting', and quiz shows such as *Ready Money* and *Tellyphonin* and chat shows in the the form of the dreadful *Friday Night Live*. Local programmes on the ITV network are more often than not aired in the late night or early afternoon ghetto slots. HTV Wales is unique amongst ITV contractors in maintaining its commitment to local current affairs by moving its award winning programme *Wales This Week* to an early-evening slot. However, this is under threat from the ITV schedulers, who seek to take the 7.30pm slot to broadcast more sport and films.

Since the retention of its franchise HTV has overall broadcast more programmes but has given the viewer less choice with an emphasis placed on cheap, local entertainment programmes. It should not be forgotten that BBC Wales is also concerned with entertainment. It produces on average 5 hours of sport per week, including highly choreographed, pompous trailers for sports events aimed at uniting the people of Wales around a 'national' sporting occasion. But besides this self-conscious Boy's Own stuff, much of the increased investment by BBC Wales has been in worthy, 'auntie knows best' material such as *The Slate*, a smug, self-satisfied programme, whose appeal is narrow and limited and the style of which is more akin to a public information announcement for the arts than a critical review of the media, lesiure and arts activities in Wales. The increased number of 'history men' in BBC Wales has led the programme-makers to spend more time looking back to the past than forward to the emergence of a new Wales. The studio discussion has also featured prominently — bringing the chattering classes into a studio is of course cheap and cosy. As a result the Welsh viewer is caught between 'pap' and 'patrician' broadcasting with the space to represent the changing realities of daily life in Wales disappearing.

There has been a marked failure by both channels to represent Wales to the rest of the UK. HTV supplied fewer programmes to the network in 1994 than in the previous year and much of what was supplied was from the West of England, including drama series such as *Poldark* and *Wycliffe* and children's programmes such as *The Famous Five*. The company is also obsessed with developing programmes for new media outlets such as cable and satellite.[19] BBC Wales has also seen a decline in its contribution to UK network television. In 1990-91 it produced 71 hours of material for the network compared with 23 hours in 1993-94. According to the BBC Wales Controller things are now starting to look up with the Corporation's new commitment to regional programming. In 1994 it was announced that £75 million would be spent on regional programme-making with Cardiff identified as a 'centre of excellence' for the production of music. The new money has seen an increase in drama, produced by BBC Wales for network as well as for local audiences. BBC Wales's network productions have been criticised. John Osmond[20] points out the high profile production, *Oliver's Travels* , made by BBC Wales for network, had little if anything to do with representing Wales to the rest of Britain. Similiar criticism can be applied to *Lifeboat*, the other major drama from BBC Wales. This perhaps highlights a problem with the *British* Broadcasting Corporation's regional policy — it is less to do with the production of programmes that represent life in the regions and more to do with shifting London programmes and programme-making values out to regional centres. Welsh programme-makers rightly point to London management's resistance to and prejudice against things Welsh — recently illustrated by the fact that in the year August 1995 to 1996, only 0.2% of Channel Four's output was commissioned from Welsh independent companies. A recent *Sunday Times* article highlighted the 'anti -Welsh' bias of British broadcasting.[21] But sometimes London's prejudices are used as an excuse to cover up problems closer to home. Questions have to be raised about the ability of BBC Wales and HTV to 'sell' and present themselves to the network. There is also a confusion over the best way to represent Welshness.

There are difficulties in finding a set or sets of distinct images of Wales to represent Wales to its own people and to the outside world. Many English-speakers in Wales see the need to sustain television in two languages as depriving them of a full and comprehensive service. In some quarters the 'Welsh language lobby' is seen as a weight around the neck of those who are trying to get programmes about Wales on the network and to reach the international audience. Wales's leading film director, Karl Francis, is apoplectic in his denunciation of the influence of the language. It is the 'Baal of Welsh film and television' and 'its followers slaves of pagan dreams. Sick dreams'.[22] Francis in the midst of his tirade does raise the issue of patronage but this is something that faces the artist/film maker in all cultures. More to the point is the complexity of Welsh identity.

National identities are riven with contradictions provided by the experience of racial, social, linguistic, gender and age divisions, to mention but a few. The power to define Welshness has been at the centre of the debate about the role of the media in Welsh society. The media, for example, like other Welsh institutions, are dominated by middle-aged men, who often hanker after the good old days of the heavy, dirty industries and sing the praises of their team at Cardiff Arms Park. Their Wales is not in keeping with modern Welsh society which has far more women on low wages in service industries than men in traditional employment. People in North Wales complain about the southern bias in the Welsh media — 'Radio Rhondda' as some of them call Radio Wales — while critical voices have been raised about the portrayal of 'twp' Northerners in S4C's long-running soap, *Pobol y Cwm*.[23] Ethnic groups in Wales are virtually absent in media representations of our community. And so on. In response to the raising of 'many Welsh voices' the easy option is to fall back on the stereotypes of Welshness — and media

24

practitioners in Wales are as capable of reproducing these stereotypes as are the London media. Karl Francis, recently elevated to be head of drama at BBC Wales, has been one of the few film-makers to try to tackle what is going on in Wales today — his one-off production *Streetlife* even brought what many other Welsh film and TV makers misguidedly yearn for, favourable comments from London critics. Francis is now producing a twice-weekly soap opera, *Tiger Bay*, for BBC 1 which is supposed to be broadcast in 1997. Let's hope the multilingual and cultural diversity of Wales will be represented. Rather than see this effort as an opportunity to 'project' English-speaking Wales, a range of Welshness should be on offer, including the Welsh language which is a reality of life in this part of the world.

Such a discussion of the role of drama in representing identity is anathema to some. Reference is made to the drama output of Welsh television being 'saddled with a representational burden'.[24] To describe the artist or writer as struggling with the 'burden' of representation illustrates a lack of confidence in Wales and Welsh culture. Writers and artists should feel able to speak unself-consciously from and about their culture. The intervention of a mission to directly represent Wales can get in the way of good art and does us no favours in the long term. Makers of TV drama in Wales are handicapped by the shortage of cash. Often the grand objectives of Welsh TV drama have to be realised at a cost well below the average cost for television drama. The result is that the end-product can look 'cheap and half-realised, especially to an audience raised on sophisticated production values'.[25] The main problem of the Welsh TV nation as a whole is the economic circumstances of contemporary broadcasting and film making.

Where's the money?

The cultural mission of Welsh television has to be anchored in the economic realities of the day. There is less money and fewer resources in Welsh broadcasting today to make programmes. HTV has to pay the Treasury around £20 million per annum for the privilege of operating its franchise — nearly £1.5 million each month. The result has been cost-cutting and restructuring. Staff levels at the beginning of the 1990s were reduced to below the figure the company itself stated was necessary to provide a quality service to the TV audience in Wales and the West. The news operation in North Wales was affected by a cutback in reporters and the closure of the studio at Mold. Recently news and current affairs in HTV Wales have been able to claw back some of the lost resources as the company has begun to show strong profits — £7.3million pre-tax for 1994. News gathering was enhanced by the introduction of digital circuits which allows material to be injected directly from Carmarthen. But still the whole operation is subject to financial restrictions. Spending is carefully scrutinised by accountants who often appear the main arbiters of what is shown. This reflects the 'new commercial order' that pervades HTV. The company is today much more concerned about its reputation with the City than with the people of Wales. Its recent involvement with a consortium bidding for the new Channel 5 franchise was a clear example of the new priorities. Channel 5 will not be available to most people in Wales. The bid was put together with little or no consultation with programme-makers and the impact on the channel's commitment to regional programme-making was never discussed.

There must be increasing doubts about HTV's commitment to regional programme-making. Its Chief Executive, Chris Rowlands, trumpets that HTV 'intends to be a global player in world broadcasting'. He speaks warmly about 'rights division', now branded as Harvest, which is identified as the most dynamic part of HTV's future plans. This part of HTV's enterprises concerns film production — including the box-office comedy success *Dumb and Dumber* — as well as natural history film-makers Partridge Films who sell their programmes to companies around the world. HTV has made the 'biggest strides' recently in the area of new media such as cable and satellite — it now supplies programmes for cable channels in Britain, including Avon Cable and Windsor Cable, as well as the Discovery Channel.

While the financial pressures on programmes-makers are not as

26

great as they were at the time of the franchise renewal, there must be doubt as to how far the increased profits of the company are being ploughed back into regional programme-making. Rowlands has told his employees that the City does not see regional broadcasting as a money-making venture. He and senior echelons of the company are increasingly less enthusiastic about making programmes for Wales and the West of England. The growing indifference to the 'region' is reflected in the recent Independent Television Commission (ITC) performance review. The ITC states that 'HTV West's overall performance was weakened by the high proportion of co-productions with other ITV licensees and with satellite channels' which 'had the effect of diluting regionality and, in some cases, quality'. Viewers in the West Country 'had difficulty in identifying the regionality of HTV West's service' and saw much of the output as 'uninspiring'. The service of HTV Wales compared favourably with that for the West of England with its audience being 'served very well throughout 1995 in terms of range and quality of regional programming'. But how long can HTV Wales resist the pressure inside the company that works against the quality of its regional service?

On the surface the recent commitment to increase the money for programme making from £11 to £20 million indicates a healthy financial situation in BBC Wales. However, in the last couple of years the BBC has been subject to vast restructuring. The 'Birt revolution' is about 'downsizing, delayering and outsourcing'; in other words lay-offs, close-downs and cutbacks. It remains to be seen, despite London's greater commitment to programme making in the BBC's national regions, how long BBC Wales can maintain its rate of expansion. Morale inside the BBC — and in BBC Wales — is low. Despite more money to make programmes, more obstacles confront programme makers. Many are on short-term contracts which inhibits the risk-taking that is associated with creativity and quality television. Much of their time is spent working on the byzantine financial system developed in the wake of the introduction of 'Producer Choice'. The BBC Wales Controller's explanation for the poor staff morale inside his organization is the 'speed' at which the new system was introduced. Admitting that 'inevitable flaws' are part of any new system, he is now happy that things are 'settling down' and stresses that the new system has made producers happy because it has given them control of their own budgets.[26] This is the stuff of good public relations. At the same time as our Controller pushes out Birtist platitudes, other former senior people in the BBC bewail the changes that are still taking place. Take one example — the much respected former head of BBC World Service, John Tusa. He is outspoken in his criticism of the Birtist 'mission to destroy all those programme-led, broadcasting-led structures that made good programmes and satisfied huge audiences against tough competition at home and abroad'[27]. Tusa is not the only BBC critic to use the words of anonymous BBC programme-makers complaining about the negative impact of devolved budgets on the process of making programmes. He —along with many others — also sees the new BBC regional policy as a sham: 'in practice the only beneficiaries have not been the audience but the bureaucrats policing the system and British Rail's Intercity as producers and presenters roam the regional headquarters of the BBC making programmes that are truly regional in name only'. This contrasts with the more sanguine public view taken by the BBC Wales Controller of the merits of BBC regional policy. Then again he has to be more optimistic, doesn't he?

But it is not simply a case of a financial squeeze and commercial reorganization in the broadcast world. In Wales as elsewhere in Europe there has been a shift from the concept of public service to market forces as the basis for running broadcasting. Deregulation has meant that broadcasting is driven more and more by the market. This is most apparent in the ITV sector since the changes brought about by the Thatcher government in 1990. Broadcasters must now produce the kinds of programmes that maximise the audience that can be delivered to advertisers. The BBC financial base is supposedly protected by the licence fee. But with pressure from government on the licence fee the BBC, in order to justify the fee, is also having to show it can gather large audiences for its programmes. Hence the pressure throughout British and Welsh broadcasting is towards more entertainment programmes such as soaps and quiz programmes which bring in viewers in large numbers. The BBC has recently been allowed to develop advertising, which further undermines the licence fee. The more the Corporation shows that it can raise funds from commercial ventures, the less justification there is for public support through the levy of the licence fee. But the crucial impact of deregulation is on how broadcasters view their audience. The pressures on broadcasters today are to see viewers not as citizens but as consumers. The new credo is to maximise audience ratings by giving people what they want. Considerations of what they need and what is needed to build a healthy and vibrant citizenship and community are downplayed. While there was a lot wrong with Reith and Reithian values, the great strength of this vision of broadcasting was that it had a social conscience which went beyond the simple process of satisfying people's basic wants. This should not be forgotten — and it is a shame that at a time when Wales needs such a vision it is the values of consumerism that are increasingly predominant in Welsh broadcasting. Broadcasting — as well as other media production — should be about a balance between leading as well as reflecting people's wants and needs.

Desperately seeking an audience

The output of Welsh television cannot be discussed separately from the changes in the Welsh audience since 1979. Today fewer people are watching television. As more audiovisual outlets have become available, with the development of satellite, cable and video, demand has slumped. People would rather do other things with their leisure time. It is also clear that many people in Wales still do not watch Welsh television. The removal of Welsh-language programmes from the BBC and HTV has not led to people turning back their aerials to Wales. Many viewers in South Wales, particularly in south Glamorgan, still boycott Welsh television by pointing their aerials to the Mendip transmitter. It has been estimated that as many as 55% of the households in the Vale of Glamorgan tune their aerials to HTV West rather than

HTV Wales. In Cardiff the figure is 37% and Newport 46%.[28] In North Wales HTV Wales is challenged by Granada; certain reception areas such as much of Wrexham and Deeside are not even able to pick up HTV Wales. Despite this situation there has been little effort made by either BBC Wales or HTV Wales to mount a campaign to persuade viewers to tune into Wales.

The inclination of large segments of the Welsh television audience to the West of England service is difficult to explain. It is made all the more difficult if you pay attention to the ITC Performance Report which states that the quality of programmes provided by HTV Wales is better than that provided by HTV West. Why do people in Wales tune into a service which gives them local news and current affairs about Bristol and the West? The answer lies partly in the laziness of many people in getting around to changing their aerials and the cost involved — a lesson for those pushing the new digital technology — as well as the traditional hostility to the Welsh-language service. But there are also problems in answering this question. Very little is known about the habits of the television audience in Wales. Audience research is limited to the broadcasting institutions who jealously guard their ratings. The only piece of recent qualitative research into the Welsh TV audience indicates that people in Wales still regard their local programmes as being of 'poor quality' in relation to network production. The study completed for the Institute of Welsh Affairs in 1990 also found that people throughout Wales wanted more 'serious' programming about Wales such as news and current affairs, documentaries and natural history programmes. While there is perhaps a more catholic range of interests amongst Welsh viewers, *Broadcast* magazine in its survey of Welsh viewing habits found that soap operas do even better in Wales than in other parts of the United Kingdom.[29] It is also perhaps a poignant reflection on Welshness that S4C's highest rated programme in 1994 was the American film *Misery*.

However, the most interesting finding concerned attitudes to an English-language channel for Wales. The idea for such a channel came out of the scramble for the ITV franchise and in February 1990 *The Western Mail* found that 73% of people in

Wales would be 'in favour of Wales having its own television channel to serve the English-speakers in the same way that S4C serves Welsh-speakers'. The Institute of Welsh Affairs survey found a similar number of people supporting the idea of such a channel (65%) but of these only 63% said they would watch the channel very much. Support for such a channel was also much stronger amongst Welsh-speakers, the younger age-group, the C1s and C2s and people in Gwent and Mid Glamorgan. The desirability of such a channel varied considerably throughout Wales, reflecting what the report referred to as 'the general disunity of Wales — geographically and culturally'.[30] The present policy of offering English-language Welsh programme opt-outs on BBC and ITV, based on the findings of this research, is likely to produce more people watching programmes about Wales in English than a dedicated English-language channel for Wales.

English-speakers are not the only part of the Welsh broadcasting audience who feel that their needs and wants are not fully catered for. Some mention has already been made of how other parts of the audience, for example, people in North Wales, ethnic groups, women and working people, are treated. It is interesting to note that more ABC1 viewers make up S4C's audience than even that of Channel Four. But most significant is that young people in Wales are increasingly seeing themselves as marginalised. The problems of trying to adjust the output to meet the needs of a younger audience are illustrated by Radio Cymru's recent radical changes to cater for younger viewers. The introduction of more music, including English-language music, and items with a greater appeal to a younger audience, has elicited a backlash from the traditional audience. For linguistic purists the introduction of English-language music is the thin end of a wedge while others are critical of the introduction of 'silly chat and music' at the expense of talk. As the new voice of Radio Cymru, disc-jockey Eifion Jones says the new format is 'tabloid radio' and 'it's not about issues — it's light entertainment'.[31] Changes in BBC Radio Wales and Radio Cymru have to been seen in terms of the deregulation of radio. Since the late 1980s there has been a proliferation of radio stations throughout Wales and the rest of the British Isles. From Marcher Coast FM in North Wales and Radio Ceredigion in West Wales to Red Dragon Radio in Cardiff and Swansea Sound, the BBC in Wales has seen increased competition. In the face of such competition the BBC has either had to respond by producing material of a 'more commercial nature', going 'downmarket' and providing less 'serious' progamming and more 'light entertainment'. Radio Wales has repositioned itself by stressing more serious talk alongside the likes of Roy Noble — a kind of Radio Four for the Welsh. The commercial realities of the new commerical order in radio in Wales means that the broadcasters are forced to respond to the viewers primarily through the mechanism of the market, which means undermining an all-Wales agenda at the expense of locality and promoting cheap entertainment at the expense of more challenging material. This is a very narrow judgement as to what the audience wants.

In terms of providing a voice for Wales, broadcasting agencies are today confronted by a number of problems. There is a commitment from Welsh broadcasting organizations to developing national consciousness and reporting the national agenda. This is reflected in the increase in programmes about and for Wales. However, the changing economic foundations of broadcasting are making it more difficult to produce programmes of quality which can cater for the diversity of Welshness. The focus on entertainment at the expense of information can be seen as undermining democracy in Wales. There are fewer resources to scrutinise those institutions responsible for running people's lives. The huge growth of quangos in Wales has not been matched by a corresponding growth in the resources and effort devoted by the media to the investigation of these institutions. At least local councils in Wales — the elected quangos of yesterday — were subjected to aggressive investigation by the magazine *Rebecca*. If a healthy democracy is measured by the extent of informed debate, then Wales is less democratic today than twenty years ago. The quality of information flowing into the public domain has declined as journalism and broadcasting have become increasingly undernourished.

The lack of accountability of everyday Welsh media folk

The problems that face the Welsh media are not simply a matter of structures, finance and audience. There is also a question of the commitment and ability of those who work in the media, especially those responsible for the operation of the press and broadcasting, to the development of a Welsh agenda. In the case of the press there appears to have been little concern from owners about the relationship of their newspapers to Wales. The Thomson Corporation, which up until the end of 1995 owned *The Western Mail* and a number of major evening and local titles in Wales, was very distant from the running of its Welsh newspapers. Their main concern was that their subsidiary in Britain, Thomson Regional Newspapers (TRN), would generate revenue to finance other of the conglomerate's interests. In 1996 the Welsh newspapers were sold to Trinity, a newspaper group closer to home, based in Cheshire. Trinity now controls all the major newspapers in Wales. The group has paid attention to increasing its profitability through takeovers and mergers, the constant drive for more low-cost production, including low labour costs with the rationalisation of the news collection process. Accountability is first and foremost to the profit-sheet and the shareholder, not the community and the public.

Welsh broadcasting is a very incestuous industry with fathers and sons, fathers and daughters, uncles and nephews as well as friends of the family working in it. The closeness of the ties between those who work at the top of television, for example, can be seen as producing a mindset that in some ways deadens creativity. The Broadcasting Council for Wales, the body responsible for the BBC's public accountability, is drawn from a narrow base. This has led to some embarrassing moments in recent times for the BBC in Wales. In May 1994 a BBC Wales *Week In Week Out* investigation examined the involvement of the Welsh Development Agency with Cynon Valley Borough Council in a land deal in Aberdare. After the programme was shown, the Broadcasting Council discussed its content which was heavily criticised. Chairing the meeting was Dr. Gwyn Jones, formerly the head of the WDA and one of the members present was Tony Roberts, Chief Executive of Cynon Valley Borough Council. It could be argued that the lack of representativeness of the Council in this case could have threatened the integrity of BBC Wales's journalism.[32]

But in a more general sense it raises questions about the relationship between broadcasters and the Welsh public. The public have over the years been excluded from public service broadcasting in Britain. The BBC serves the 'good and great' who are appointed to the councils responsible for ensuring the representation of the public interest. The ITC Viewers' Consultative Council for Wales is no different. In 1990 the Council consisted of the wife of a Labour MP, a manager of a private firm, a former prison governor, a trade union official, a former under-sheriff, a local councillor who was 'a Guide and Brownie leader', a lecturer who 'sang in two local choirs', a former mayor of Neath, a public affairs manager who was a 'keen sportsman', a farmer's wife 'active in the W.I.', a borough councillor and mother of a young son, and the organiser of the only police studies training course in the U.K.. The deliberations of these councils are not open to public scrutiny and nobody really knows what they are saying about programmes on behalf of the Welsh public. The BBC in recent years has recognised the importance of being more representative — the failure to mobilise public support for the Corporation in the face of the Thatcher onslaught brought home to them the need to be more in touch with the public. But there is still the question of how bodies, such as the Council, gauge the public's views on programmes, other than using the facts and figures compiled by the broadcasters themselves. In the early 1980s one member of the Council told me he simply asked his family and his secretary what they thought of programmes. Such is the process of finding out what people think about broadcasting in Wales!

The deregulation of broadcasting has increased the power of one shadowy group of broadcasters — commissioning editors. HTV and BBC Wales, in line with government requirements, commission more and more programmes from independent

34

sources. As S4C does not make any of the programmes it broadcasts, these nameless and faceless people exercise even more power in Welsh-language television. The commissioning process is shrouded in mystery. How do you become a commissioning editor? What attributes do you need for the job? How are programmes commissioned? What criteria do commissioning editors use for selection? Friends, family, people they used to work with? What are the penalties for commissioning programmes nobody watches or listens to? How and when do these people talk to the public, defend their decisions, and generally make themselves accountable to their audience? Who knows!

All change with a wired-up Wales?

New media technology threatens to shift the debate about the role of the Welsh media to another level. This technology comes in a bewildering array of forms. Cable, satellite, digital, the electronic newsroom, the internet, home computer games, on-line data bases, e-mail and the C-D Rom are some examples of the new technology. How all these impact on the development of the mass media is problematic and as yet far from clear. But they will have an effect. Speculation as to the nature of the effect is rife — by and large such speculation has focused on the technology and what it can do, with a 'gee whiz' analysis that places emphasis on the positive contribution of the technology. Thus there is much talk about more channels, more information, more choice, better and more rapid communication and so on. There is less talk about the quality of channels, information and choice. Technophiles argue that we, the people, are going to be liberated from the heavy hand of the media gatekeepers who have guided our television nation since its inception in the 1950s. At last we are going to be able to talk to each other for the first time and say what we want to say without the intervention of the media gatekeepers. Technology presents the pathway to real diversity, it is said.

Perhaps more caution should be taken with speculating over these developments. Technology will change our media world but, as history shows, new media technologies have not always changed things in the way in which the pundits have envisaged. And at this point in time it is more important to focus not on what technology is doing to society but what society is doing with the new technology. After all, technology is not a given. Its uses and applications are dependent on and an outcome of decisions made by society. How cable, satellite, the internet or digital technology develop is shaped by the circumstances under which they are introduced. At present, these circumstances are dominated by the market and the overwhelming search for profit. In the brave new market world any notion of social responsibility must be strongly fought for against those who seek to use new media to sell us all manner of things weird and wonderful. The Broadcasting Bill introducing the digital era into Britain has been little debated outside Parliament — with the exception of the rumpus over the rights to cover major sporting events. Yet — as the BBC Wales Controller highlighted in his speech to the Celtic Film Festival in Bangor in 1996 — this legislation threatens to fundamentally alter the status quo in British broadcasting and sweep away the present broadcasting landscape of Wales.

The new technology comes in the shape of megabits, multiplexes and compressions — all of which are enough to give the layperson a headache. The upshot is that the technology holds forth the promise of more channels and a wider service. More radio and more television channels and stations and services. This is seen as a solution to some of the problems in Welsh broadcasting, which are in part the product of the scarcity of the airwaves. All those who at present cannot receive Channel Four will through digital technology be able to see both S4C and Channel 4. The new technology also gives a reality to the possibility of a dedicated channel for non-Welsh-speaking Welsh people. But the framework being developed under the Broadcasting Bill holds — potentially — as many problems as it promises to resolve. In particular, the radical change in the position of S4C which has been given the opportunity of developing new services as a result of the allocation of digital space. Lucky Wales. But how is S4C going to fill the new space?

36

Not with programmes from Channel Four which it now receives free but may be deprived of under the new legislation. Co-operation with the private sector, such as cable and satellite operators, could be a possibility. But this of course would result in increased costs and increased commercialisation of the channel which could threaten its mission to preserve Welsh culture. Or more programmes could be provided by BBC Wales which at present contributes 10.5 hours of news and current affairs per week free? Or perhaps more English-language programmes which changes in S4C's remit under the Bill will now allow it to broadcast? But the financial squeeze on programme-making at both the BBC and HTV will again mean that increased production from this quarter is problematic and costly. Much is made of the opportunities of independent producers to fill the schedule. While the independent production sector in Wales is relatively strong, it is not strong enough to produce a range of quality programmes required by the new channel. There is a dilemma for Welsh broadcasting brought about by the new technology — as the BBC Wales Controller recognised in his Bangor speech, the present situation is 'pregnant with opportunities, yet fraught with dangers'.[33] How to tackle these changes is crucial to the development of the Welsh media system. More genuine public debate and more consideration throughout the media in Wales is vital if the present growth of media made in Wales is to continue.

What is to be done?

In this final section I shall make some suggestions for change. These are made by someone — as it will no doubt be pointed out — who does not work in the media. They are therefore confined to addressing the role of the media in their broader relationship with Welsh society. Programme-making, for example, is a matter for the programme makers   although the views of members of the audience are not without import in this area. However, media production in general takes place within a broader environment which shapes not only what is shown and said but also fuels the creative endeavours of the film maker, writer and television programme maker. There are important aspects of this broader environment in Wales which could be changed.

Make S4C a national asset

Welsh broadcasting is too important to be left to BBC Wales and HTV Cymru/Wales — the former is too much a tool of the whims of a centralised, London-centric media organization while the other is increasingly steeped in a market structure which pays little heed to the needs of regions. The importance of S4C to the future development of Welsh broadcasting is crucial. S4C's importance has often been underestimated. Many English-speakers — particularly those with aspirations to make television programmes — are forthright in their criticism of the channel. 'Telly for the daft', they say, as they moan about the poor quality of what is put out by S4C. To some extent they have a point — often Welsh-language programme makers are unimaginative, happy to peddle the emblematic and reinforce stereotypes of Welshness. But it is also fair to point out that throughout British television the viewer can switch on to be greeted with trash. There has always been bad television — Groucho Marx commented in the 1960s that they 'recycle their rubbish in California and call it television'. Today the problem is that there is more rubbish and it is not confined to S4C. What is forgotten is the important contribution that S4C has made to the development of the Welsh media and Welsh life.

The importance of S4C's contribution to the cultural regeneration of Wales cannot be underestimated. Sitting in the middle of Wales's media landscape, it has helped to galvanise other areas of Welsh cultural life. It has provided confidence to Welsh-speaking endeavours, either by televising events or giving outlets to artists to express themselves. The channel has directly and indirectly, through financial and non-financial means, enabled the laying down of a platform to support cultural production in Wales. This is most apparent in the growth of a relatively healthy independent media production sector in Wales. But other smaller scale cultural outlets have benefitted. It is also the case that English-language cultural production in Wales has been assisted. Take television current affairs. This is stronger in Wales than many other regions of Britain — as well as Europe. Both BBC Wales and HTV support respectively *Week In Week Out* and *Wales This Week*, which have high production values as well as maintaining the tradition of investigative journalism. It was the birth of S4C, with the remit to provide current affairs in Welsh, that brought into being *Wales This Week* and enabled *Week In Week Out* to thrive. Both the money and commitment from the new channel were crucial but, above all, it was the embarrassment factor that proved an incentive to the successful expansion of English-language current affairs programmes for Wales.

However, the Welsh-language focus of the channel is a source of much controversy. In certain parts of Wales S4C is received instead of Channel Four UK — in Gwent, for example, where nearly 98% of the population do not speak Welsh. This led to a campaign for the provision of Channel Four, in the midst of which S4C was charged with being insensitive to the needs of those deprived of their Channel Four. This charge is somewhat unfair given that S4C reschedules Channel Four programmes outside peak hours — only 34 hours per week of Welsh programmes are provided. But there are problems with the ability of S4C to reschedule the Channel Four programmes at regular and convenient times. Much aggravation has been caused by this failure of scheduling. The real dilemma for the channel is the extent of its commitment to serving all Wales rather than Welsh-speakers. From the outset the tension between language and nation has been apparent. Early efforts to represent the bilingual and multicultural nature of Welsh society, programmes such as *Bowen a'i Bartner*, were criticised by 'linguistic purists' who regarded them as slipping from the remit of the channel to serve the Welsh language. Matters came to a head over the launch by S4C of its early-evening magazine programme, *Heno*, produced by an independent company and broadcast not from the traditional base of Welsh-language independents, Gwynedd and Cardiff, but from Swansea. *Heno* was established to appeal to the working-class Welsh-speakers of industrial South Wales, by using 'street Welsh' and a mixture of Welsh and English. The move was criticised by traditionalists who condemned the channel for lowering standards. However, S4C has made considerable efforts to breach the linguistic divide in Wales: over 50% of the channel's output is now subtitled in English and a subtitling service has been designed for Welsh learners.

But if S4C has taken a number of important steps towards reaching out to the Wales beyond the Welsh-speaking community, it still has not gone far enough to making itself fully committed to cultural production throughout the whole of Wales. The opportunity to provide a fully comprehensive service for the whole nation is possibly within the grasp of S4C as a result of new technology. But the ability to seize the opportunity lies in the hands of those in charge. Are they able to make the necessary changes? These changes will involve collaboration with others in broadcasting. The BBC Wales Controller appears to welcome such collaboration. He sees closer collaboration a financial and technological necessity as well as a cultural need[34]. HTV Wales is perhaps less interested. But S4C as a public service institution and a primary purchaser of programmes is crucial. And in this sense it should take the lead, including reforming its management and governing structures to make them more representative of Wales as a whole.

A single broadcasting authority

If S4C is to actively exploit its role at the centre of the emerging Welsh media system it will have to embrace change. As the BBC Wales Controller states: 'We will not solve the three great challenges of sustaining Welsh-language broadcasting, addressing the imbalance of Welsh and English language provision, and finding our proper place in a much, much wider market-place unless we consider our problems in the round and seek collaborative solutions'[35]. But how should this take place in practice? For the Controller it is a matter of sharing facilities, co-producing programmes and co-operating in the financing of production services and programmes. This is fine in intent but messy in practice. It also focusses at the level of tactical awareness rather than strategy and vision, which is what is desperately needed in Welsh broadcasting today. For some this can only be provided by the establishment of a single broadcasting authority for Wales.

If a Welsh Assembly ever comes into being, one of the areas in which it could exert some degree of influence is cultural and media issues. The breaking up of those quangos responsible for broadcasting in Wales is to be welcomed. Unelected, unaccountable and unrepresentative, the Broadcasting Council and the ITC in Wales serve no one but the small elite of time-servers who sit on them. What's required is a genuinely representative and accountable regulatory body that could oversee the output and performance of the broadcasting services in Wales as well as co-ordinate the growth of a 'holistic' view of Welsh broadcasting. The development of a blueprint for the Welsh broadcasting media, as well as what it is trying to achieve in the provision of entertainment, information and education for a Welsh audience, should be the remit of such an authority.

The setting up of such a body will not be easy. Traditional animosity between Welsh and English broadcasters and audiences militate against the integration of broadcasting in a single authority. If the authority were to be established by an Assembly of local councillors then there must be questions about its representativeness and accountability. Such a body will have to represent a range of opinion, interests and expertise within Wales as well as respond to public and popular debate. Such a model for democratic broadcasting accountability is not to be found in Britain. However, across the channel in Europe, in countries such as Holland and Belgium, models for genuine representative, accountable and responsive broadcasting authorities are to be found. These models have also been evolved in the context of providing a service in two languages.

41

A media charter for Wales

Structures, however, cannot be divorced from people. It is people who make programmes, produce papers and magazines and listen, read and watch. A new environment needs to be established that will provide the opportunity for creativity and risk-taking in the broadcasting and print media. In a recent speech, one of the elder statesmen of Welsh and British broadcasting, Geraint Stanley Jones, came up with the idea of a broadcasting charter. Steeped in the Reithian tradition that broadcasting should reflect and shape the life of the nation, he believes that such a document is a vital part of 'getting our Welsh act together' in the face of the radical changes that are taking place. The 'Broadcasting Manifesto for the Millenium' should examine the aims, structures, technology and, above all, programmes'[36]. Stanley Jones's suggestion could be extended to an examination of all media in Wales — after all, we are told that the future will be interactive and the differences and distinctions between media forms blurred. A Media Charter for Wales could take a broad view of what the role of the media should be in the contemporary situation and address the best way to develop our mass media to benefit the people of Wales. Bringing practitioners together to discuss such matters could also result in a productive exchange of views and experiences as well as stimulating thoughts, ideas and even actions about the kinds of programmes and products that could best serve the needs of modern Wales and the Welsh audience. But any such discussion must take into account the views of the ordinary viewers, listeners and readers.

Access to the media

Broadcasters, print journalists, film-makers are all in a relationship with their audience. It is impossible to understand the content of the mass media without understanding the nature of this relationship. However, this relationship is an imaginary one, a construction that operates within the minds of the media practitioner and the traditions of the media institution that he or she works for. Media people have little or no direct contact with their audience. At most their point of contact is through ratings or circulation figures, or feedback from audience research or letters from those who have the energy to pick up the pen to write in about what they see, hear or read. These ways of contact are all artificial and unrepresentative. They only provide a minimal insight into the range of views, wants and needs of the audience. Of course it is no easy matter to find out what the mass of people think or want. As a result, most people working in the media have a mental image of their reader, their viewer or their listener. A stereotype is constructed of the *The Western Mail* reader or *The Slate* viewer or the *Wales This Week* viewer or the listener who tunes into Roy Noble on Radio Wales. This reductionist construction plays an important part in determining the nature of the product that is served up.

Such a view of the relationship between the media practitioner and the audience is often dismissed by those working in the media. They say that people like their product, otherwise they wouldn't buy newspapers or watch television. This presupposes that there is a real choice in the media market-place. The monopoly of media outlets in many parts of the market-place — which the logical outcome of competition and the drive for profit and efficiency — means that often viewers, listeners and readers do not have a real choice. Where else can you turn in Cardiff for an evening newspaper if you can't find anything to read in the *South Wales Echo*? Even if there is a competing outlet, it does not often mean there is a choice of product. Take the example of radio stations in Wales — increasingly what is on offer, with perhaps the exception of a few stations such as Bay FM in Cardiff and Radio Ceredigion, is the same mixture of popular music, ads and jingles and gossip pumped out by the different stations. The trend to homogeneity in the content of media brought about by market forces is based on particular assumptions about the audience — readers, viewers and listeners are above all treated as consumers. Without more knowledge of what the audience wants there is limited room to challenge this conceptualisation of who is the audience. More access to newspaper pages and the airwaves is required as well as to those who make programmes and edit newspapers.

At the outset, access to the channel for the S4C audience was not a problem, as the channel had been born out of the struggles of that audience. However, feedback mechanisms, including regular public meetings and programmes such as *Spectrwm* and *Ar y Bocs* came and went very quickly. Broadcasters in Wales point to the poor attendance at public meetings arranged by them as an indication of either public apathy or satisfaction with what they are broadcasting. Meetings set up in dingy community halls after work on a winter's evening are hardly conducive to encouraging public participation in the media. And this is what the role of the broadcasting authorities should be — to encourage popular involvement. The general indifference to such an objective was highlighted during the last round of awarding new ITV franchises in 1990. The ITC, the body responsible for representing the voice of the public, declined to organise any public meetings so that the viewers could hear the proposals of the different applicants. Broadcasting in Britain started as a local service with public participation. The rise of professionalism in the industry has been at the expense of the audience. This trend needs to be arrested if the Welsh media are to play a fuller role in the building of identity and citizenship in Wales. Some public access does exist at a banal level — BBC 2's *Video Nation*, BBC Wales's *Answering Back* and the plethora of candid camera type programmes. But more thought should be given to how to integrate the audience into the decision making process. Right of reply programming as well as space for people to express their own views under their own editorial control must be considered. In addition the audience should have some form of representation within the structures of broadcasting — at least at the outset on the bodies charged with exercising public accountability in the industry.

Training for popular television

Some of these suggested changes are unapologetically idealistic. Those working in the media will no doubt say these suggestions are unrealistic, flying in the face of the way the world is. Perhaps they are. But ideals are important: something to aim at is an essential part of any endeavour in life. Today's media workers are trapped in an environment which does not allow them to breathe. Creativity is controlled by the money men and women. Risk is not encouraged and obligations to anything beyond the ratings and ensuring that you do not make mistakes are discouraged. But also young people entering the industry are not pushed to raise their heads and set their sights on broader social responsibilities. Trained to push buttons, write in a particular house-style, they are fast being turned into 'tin men and women'. It is noticeable that 'good writing' is something that increasingly counts for less on training courses. Orwell was right in his assessment that good writing is a product of having something to say — perhaps they don't have much to say. Too many entering the profession today simply dream of having their faces on screen or their names in print. But journalists, broadcasters and film makers have always played a public role which brings responsibilities as well as privileges. Editors who try to tell us to believe there is no distinction between selling a Mars bar and a newspaper are fundamentally wrong — and out of touch with the roots of their profession and industry.

Journalism and programme-making need to be 're-educated' to discover their roots in the community. After all, journalism developed hand-in-hand with the growth of public opinion. It was anchored within a community and spoke for this community. The training of Welsh journalists and programme-makers needs to assert the fact that Wales is a society, culture and polity with its own values and traditions. This should be part of the training in both the English and Welsh language, although there is not enough of the latter. There should also be a reappraisal of 'popular' journalism and programme-making. The distinction drawn between 'tabloid' and 'quality' newspapers is reflected throughout the media. On the one hand, there is the 'serious', 'worthy' and 'informative' and, on the other, the 'popular', 'entertaining' or 'trivial' — and never the twain shall meet. However, informative journalism and programme-making can be interesting and accessible while entertainment can be challenging. Journalism education should seek to develop a popular approach which is both stimulating and challenging. This means treating viewers and readers with more respect.

Local media tax

But there is a bottom line — who pays? A commercial system of financing undermines the ability and capacity of the media to play a central role in promoting Welshness and Welsh identity and citizenship. Profit comes before social responsibility. Wales never was and never will be able to sustain a commercial broadcasting and print system — it is too small, geographically dispersed and poor. It is only through some form of public service system that the media will be able to finance themselves and make a full contribution to the development of Wales. Public service must therefore be defended as the best way forward — even though the present public service institutions are in need of fundamental reform to bring them closer to the public. Public service media are at present financed through subsidy from the Department of National Heritage — primarily through the licence fee which is a poll tax levied on every individual — and a levy on ITV profits. Public funds are also channelled to the small magazine sector in Wales via the Arts Council. The present combination of finance, commercial and public, is likely to continue into the future. But it is possible for a Welsh Assembly to reassess the basis and nature of subsidy used to support the Welsh media. It is also possible to envisage a local media tax which could be levied for the purpose of either supporting access to the airwaves, or subsidising diversity in the Welsh print and magazine industry or establishing new training programmes.

A nationalist agenda?

Whatever the future of Welsh broadcasting, there needs to be more than anything else a broader debate about the role of the media in Welsh society. For some, suggestions that the media should play a more active role in promoting Welsh identity, developing citizenship in Wales and shaping Welshness are treated with mistrust — a 'nationalist agenda' is seen as lurking in the background. They are dismissed as anachronistic, a throwback to the past, and generally out of touch with the modern world with its developing global culture. However, it can be argued that the opposite is true. Increasingly, in order to compete and participate in today's world, a sense of self is important. A distinct image needs to be presented and a distinct voice needs to be heard. Wales needs to be seen and heard in this world and it is largely through the mass media that this can be most effectively done. Above all, the mass media have a part to play in encouraging our sense of self-respect as a community and people. Much is made about Wales and the Welsh accent not being 'sexy' with the London media. Our response is to complain about the prejudice of the English and trot out a list of great Welsh men and women who, we think, have 'charisma' and 'talent' and should be given more attention by the London media. But perhaps we should respond by looking more to ourselves and our inferiority complex — sometimes it seems we do not want or expect Wales and things Welsh to be taken seriously or treated with respect. Becoming 'sexy' is something that rests in our own hands, not anyone else's. The media in Wales have a crucial role in helping us to overcome our inferiority complex and developing our sense of self-respect. It is only then we will be taken seriously and on our own terms by the outside world.

FOOTNOTES

[1]Jones, Aled *Press, Politics and Society: A History of Journalism in Wales* Cardiff: University of Wales Press, 1990 p 227.

[2]see Mackay, Hughie and Powell, Tony 'Wales and Its Media: Production, Consumption and Regulation' in *Contemporary Wales* (forthcoming); Skilton, David 'More Words and Pictures in the Air' in Cole, David (ed) *The New Wales* Cardiff: University of Wales Press 1990; Talfan Davies, Geraint *Broadcasting in Wales in the Digital Age* Address to the Celtic Film and Television Festival, Bangor, Wales, March 28, 1996.

[3]quoted in Vacquero Romero, Eduardo *The Rebirth of Minority Languages through the Media: a comparative study of Wales and Luxembourg* MA dissertation in European Journalism Studies, University of Wales, Cardiff, 1995 p 46.

[4]Lucas, Rowland *The Voice of a Nation?* Llandysul: Gomer Press, 1981. p 53.

[5]Tunstall, Jeremy *The Media in Britain* London: Constable, 1983, p 228.

[6]Smith, Maurice *Paper Lions: The Scottish Press and National Identity* Edinburgh: Polygon 1994.

[7]Hume, Ian 'Mass Media and Society in the 1980s' in Hume, I & Pryce, E *The Welsh and their Country* Llandysul: Gomer Press, 1983. p 331.

[8]Evans, Martin *Television in Wales - Opinion Survey: an exploratory research programme* Cardiff: Institute of Welsh Affairs, 1992.

[9]see Williams, Kevin 'What Wales Wants is *Wales on Sunday*' *Planet* 102 December 1993/January 1994 pps 7-12 for a discussion of the development of the newspaper.

[10]Williams, Emyr *Y Papurau Bro a'r Farchnad Hysbysebu* Caerdydd: Ganolfan Gydweithredol Cymru, 1992. Mackay, Hughie and Powell, Tony *op cit* identify the total circulation of these papers as 50,000.

[11]Skilton, David *op cit* p189.

[12]Hume, Ian *op cit* p 338.

[13]Williams, Kevin *op cit* p 9.

[14]Talfan Davies, Geraint 'Broadcasting and the Nation' *Planet* 92 April-May, 1992 pps 16-22

[15]Balsom, Dennis 'Solid Support for S4C Survey' *Western Mail* February 27, 1991.

[16]quoted in Vacquero Romero, Eduardo *op cit* p 49.

[17]Betts, Clive & Basini, Mario 'Give English-speakers more TV of quality' *Western Mail* July 14, 1994.

[18]*See for Yourself* BBC Wales (Cardiff) January 7, 1991 quoted in Osmond, John *Welsh Europeans* Bridgend: Seren 1995 p 112.

[19]see HTV 'Channels for the Future' Annual Report and Accounts, 1994.

[20]Osmond, John *op cit* p 117.

[21]'Welsh wilt under yoke of television 'Taffism'' *The Sunday Times* May 12, 1996.

[22]Francis, Karl 'English is a Welsh Language Too' in R. Gerallt Jones (ed) *Tuag at y Filrif / Toward the Millennium* Gregynog: Gwasg Gregynog 1995.

[23]Griffiths, Alison '*Pobol y Cwm* : The Contruction of National and Cultural Identity in a Welsh-language Soap Opera' in Drummond, Phillip, Paterson, Richard and Willis, Janet (eds) *National Identity and Europe: The Television Revolution* London: British Film Institute 1993 pps 9-25.

[24]Blandford, Steve and Upton, Julian ' Courting the Network' *Planet* 117 June/July 1996 pps 70-76.

[25]ibid.

[26]Talfan Davies, Geraint 'Coping with Change in a Goldfish Bowl' *Planet* 113 October/November 1995 p 59.

[27]Tusa, John 'A Mission to Destroy' *The Guardian* June 10, 1996.

[28]Osmond, John 'Broadcasting TV figures' *Wales on Sunday* March 4, 1990.

[29]'Television Outside London' *Broadcast* July 28, 1995.

[30]Evans, Martin *op cit*

[31]*The Daily Post*, March, 19, 1996.

[32]For a discussion of the BBC Broadcasting Council for Wales see Patrick Fletcher 'Corporate Conscience', *The Western Mail*, March 23, 1995.

[33]Talfan Davies, Geraint *Broadcasting in Wales in the Digital Age* Address to the Celtic Film and Television Festival, Bangor, Wales, March 28, 1996.

[34]ibid

[35]ibid

[36]Stanley Jones, Geraint *Broadcasting in a New Age: a look into the broadcasting future* Address to Royal Television Society, Cardiff, November 1995.

ACKNOWLEDGEMENTS

This booklet could not have been written without the thoughts, ideas and time of a number of people. First and foremost, thanks to John Barnie of *Planet* who encouraged me to write a regular column for his magazine on the Welsh media. Writing the column has allowed me to share with the people at *Planet* some ridiculous moments with people in positions of influence in the Welsh media.

I should also like to thank John Osmond, Phil Cooke, Kevin Morgan, Hughie Mackay, Tony Powell, Stephen Evans, John Foscolo and David Miller for their willingness to share their views and opinions with me.

Finally I owe a debt of gratitude to Meic Stephens for asking me to write this booklet in his *Changing Wales* series. His patience in waiting for a manuscript as well as the time he spent correcting some of my Welsh and English was most appreciated.

Thanks also to a number of people who work in the print, broadcasting and magazine industries in Wales who have been willing to talk to me but who wish to remain anonymous.

changing **WALES**

Other titles in the series

Referendom = Yes or No ~~July~~ Sept '97
Assembly - Summer 1999...